BLOODHOOF

Gerður Kristný

BLOODHOOF
B L Ó Ð H Ó F N I R

Translated from the Icelandic
by Rory McTurk

PUBLICATIONS
2012

Published by Arc Publications
Nanholme Mill, Shaw Wood Road
Todmorden OL14 6DA, UK
www.arcpublications.co.uk

Copyright in original poems © Gerður Kristný 2012
Translation copyright © Rory McTurk 2012
Introduction copyright © Rory McTurk 2012
Copyright in this edition © Arc Publications, 2012

Design by Tony Ward
Printed by TJ International, Padstow, Cornwall

978 1908376 10 7 (pbk)
978 1908376 11 4 (hbk)
978 1908376 37 4 (ebk)

Cover image and illustrations © Alexandra Buhl / Forlagið

Blóðhófnir was originally published in 2010 by
Forlagið Publishing, Reykjavík, Iceland, by whose kind permission
the Icelandic text is reproduced in this volume.

The publishers acknowledge the financial assistance of

Bókmenntasjóður
The Icelandic Literature Fund

INTRODUCTION

Gerður Kristný's poem *Blóðhófnir* speaks in large measure for itself. Non-Scandinavian readers may find it helpful, however, to have a short introduction to the literary and mythological tradition from which it springs.

Gerður Kristný, an Icelandic poet and novelist, is here allying herself closely, but at the same time critically, with the literary tradition of her native land. Her poem is a modern Icelandic woman's response to the story of Freyr and Gerður as told in two main sources. One is the anonymous poem known as *Skírnismál* ('Words of Skírnir') or *För Skírnis* ('Skírnir's journey'), preserved in its fullest form as part of the so-called Poetic Edda in an Icelandic manuscript dating from the second half of the thirteenth century. The other source is the Prose Edda by the Icelander Snorri Sturluson (d. 1241), a guide for poets written in the first half of the thirteenth century and containing extended accounts of Old Norse mythology for the benefit of poets seeking to make use of mythological allusion. It is clear that the poem predates Snorri's work and was known to him, since he quotes briefly from it. Both the quotation and his version of the story indicate, however, that he knew the poem in a form rather different from that in which it is preserved most fully.

Skírnismál's version of the story is briefly as follows. A short prose introduction sets the scene in Ásgarður, the home of the gods. The god Freyr, looking out over all worlds from the god Óðinn's throne, sees in Giantland a beautiful maiden on her father's estate, and at once becomes lovesick. The poem begins with Freyr's servant Skírnir being sent to him to ask the reason for his distress. Freyr explains his love, but feels that it is doomed, no doubt because of the age-old antagonism between gods and giants. Skírnir obtains from Freyr his horse and magic sword, anticipating a journey across flames and mountains, and rides to Giantland. He finds Gerður's dwelling guarded by savage dogs, and asks a herdsman sitting on a nearby mound for advice. The reply is distinctly discouraging, but Gerður, hearing that the new-comer has dismounted from his horse, decides to admit him, after first voicing obscurely the fear that he is her brother's slayer – an allusion, perhaps, to earlier feuding between gods and giants. Once in her presence, Skírnir proceeds to woo her on Freyr's behalf, offering as inducements some golden apples and a magic, self-reproducing ring. When she refuses these gifts, indicating that she and her father, the giant Gymir, have no shortage of gold, Skírnir threatens her and her father with death by the sword, and proceeds to curse her, condemning her to a fate that includes gazing from an eagle's perch at the land of the dead and being plagued by a three-headed monster. Only when Skírnir begins to carve his curse in runic letters on a magic wand does Gerður finally relent: she agrees to meet Freyr in nine nights' time in a grove called Barri – a name in which the first element, *Barr-*, means 'barley', perhaps reflecting Freyr's status as a fertility god. Skírnir reports back to Freyr with the news, and the poem ends with Freyr complaining about the delay Gerður has imposed.

Snorri's prose version of the story differs from *Skírnismál* in a number of ways. It begins by saying that Gerður, the most beautiful of all women, is the daughter of Gymir and his wife Aurboða, who is of the race of mountain-giants. As in *Skírnismál*, it is from Óðinn's throne that Freyr first sets eyes on Gerður, but his love-sickness is here described as his punishment for having occupied that holy seat. Freyr will now neither sleep nor drink and refuses to talk to anyone. His father Njörður sends Freyr's servant Skírnir to him to inquire the cause of his distress. Freyr confesses his love for Gerður and intimates that he will die if she cannot be his. He urges Skírnir to go and ask for her hand in marriage on his behalf, and to override any resistance by her father. Skírnir undertakes this mission on condition that Freyr gives him his sword. There is no mention of the horse in Snorri's account, and no description of Skírnir's journey; the wooing of Gerður, moreover, which here takes the form of Skírnir asking on Freyr's behalf for her hand in marriage, is treated only briefly; there is no mention of proffered gifts or a curse. Gerður agrees to meet Freyr in nine nights' time on Barrey ('Barley Island'? or perhaps Barra in the Hebrides?), and Skírnir delivers this message to Freyr. The idea that the couple will marry when they meet is confined to Snorri's account; *Skírnismál* does not mention marriage explicitly. The story in Snorri's version ends with a stanza quoted from *Skírnismál* in which Freyr complains about the delay Gerður has imposed on their union.

Neither of these accounts answers the question of whether Freyr and Gerður actually do meet as arranged. For an answer to this question we must go to another work by Snorri, *Ynglinga saga*, the first of the sixteen prose sagas that make up his encyclopedic history of the kings of Norway, known as *Heimskringla*. Here it is told that Freyr and Gymir's daughter Gerður had a son, Fjölnir, who ruled over the Swedes at Uppsala and whose reign was one of good harvests and peace; he becomes the ancestor of the historical kings of Norway.

Skírnismál is in dialogue form, consisting of forty-two stanzas spoken by the characters. Of these, Gerður speaks only eight: two more than Freyr, it is true, but a good majority of them, twenty-five in all, are spoken by Skírnir. In Snorri's prose account, which is not much longer than the summary given above, the story is told mainly from the point of view of Freyr, and to a lesser extent that of

Skírnir. In Gerður Kristnýs poem, of which the sole speaker is her namesake, the giant-maiden Gerður, this Gerður's point of view comes fully into its own for the first time.

There have been various scholarly interpretations of the original story. One is that it portrays the quickening of the crops (with *Gerður* thought of as meaning 'an enclosed field') by the sun, represented by Skírnir ('the shining one'): the awakening of winter into spring. Long ago W. Wägner, in his book *Asgard and the Gods* (1884, p. 204), compared it to the story of the Sleeping Beauty, 'wakened to new life by the warm kiss of the sun-prince' – an idea ironically reflected in the present poem with its reference to a glass casket like that of Snow White. A more recent suggestion is that *Skírnismál* is concerned with the acquisition of power by Norwegian kings.

Skírnismál is composed in a metre known as *ljóðaháttur*, or chant metre, which makes systematic use of alliteration. Gerður Kristnýs poem echoes this metre without following it slavishly: there are frequent instances of alliteration in her poem, and also in the translation. In this bilingual edition, the reader is strongly advised to compare the translation with the original Icelandic. Those readers who know Icelandic will soon find that the translation is not a literal one, and does not reflect on a one-to-one basis the stylistic features of the original. All readers will benefit from reciting the poem to themselves in the original language. With this in mind, I give here a brief guide to Icelandic pronunciation, covering only those points that are relevant to a reading of *Blóðhófnir*; it makes no claim to overall coverage.

In pronunciation, the stress should always be on the first syllable. Vowels without acute accents over them are pronounced very much as in English, except that *a* falls somewhere between the standard English pronunciations of *father* and *fat*, and *i* is pronounced consistently as in *hit*, while *u* is pronounced as in *put* rather than *but*. In Icelandic, *y* is treated as a vowel and pronounced like *i* (also as in *hit*); *æ* is pronounced like English *eye*; *ö* like *oe* in *Goethe*; *au* like *eui* in French *feuille* (not like *au* in German *Haus*); and *ei* and *ey* like *ay* in English *day*. Vowels with acute accents are pronounced as follows: *á* like English *ow* in *how*; *é* like *ye* in *yes*; *í* and *ý* like *ee* in *seen*; *ó* like English *oh*; and *ú* like *oo* in *moon*. It should be noted that when *a* occurs before *ng* (as in *gang*, p. 110 and *fangið*, p. 120) it is pronounced like *á*, i.e. like *ow* in *how*.

As for the consonants, the two letters least familiar to novices, *þ* and *ð*, are pronounced as follows: *þ* sounds like *th* in English *thin*, and *ð* like *th* in English *that*. The consonants *b, d, h, k, m, t, v*, single *l* and single *n* are pronounced much as in English. The letter *f* is pronounced as in English *father* at the beginning of a word and before *t* (*fyki*, p. 28 and *aftur*, p. 73), but like *v* within a word between vowels

BLÓÐHÓFNIR
BLOODHOOF

Minningar

snjór sem ég þjappa
í greip
hnoða í kúlu
og kasta

Memories

snow which I press
in my hands
knead into a ball
and throw

Það hendir aðeins
í huga mér

but only
in my mind

Hér festir ekki snjó

snow does not settle here

Brúin spennist
úr iðandi grasi
í gráan mökk

The bridge reaches out
from waving grass
into smoky grey cloud

Þar er landið mitt
vafið náttkyrri værð
steypt í stálkaldan ís

There is my country
wrapped in calm of night
steeped in steel-cold ice

Hér situr tungl
yfir dölum og ám

Here the moon watches
over valleys and rivers

20

Heima yfir
hrolldjúpum gljúfrum

in my homeland, over chasms
of dizzying steepness

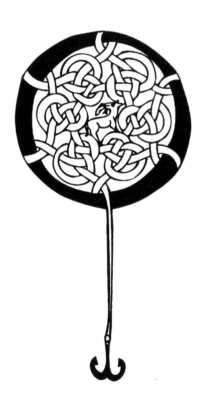

Ég sökkti öngli
í vorstillt vatn

Down went my fishhook
into water calmed by spring

Skýjaflekar
flutu um himin

Sólin í djúpinu
kveikti glit
í gárum

Rafts of cloud
floated through the sky

The sun in the depths
lit a glitter
in the ripples

Það glampaði
á augu mín
í vatninu

og festina
um háls mér

festi úr föðurást

illumining
my eyes
in the water

and the chain
round my neck

father's love in each link

Hrygna í lygnu
lék sér í
spegilmynd minni

fór inn um eyra
út um hitt

A spawner was sporting
in my image reflected
in the still water

no sooner in one ear
than out the other

Þá barst hnegg
um skóga
þagnaði fugl
faldi sig mús

dimmdi á
miðjum degi

Then came a neigh
a whinny through the woods
birds fell silent
mice ran for cover

at noon fell
a darkness

líkt og sandur fyki
yfir sveitir
og settist á lyng og lauf

as if sand were blowing
over hill and dale, settling
on leaf and ling

Skírnir
hvessti á mig
augun

Skírnir, the shining one,
fixed me
with his gaze

Hestur hans
reistur
og rífur á vöxt

Dökkur á lit
líkt og höggvinn
úr myrkri

His horse
of ample stature
stood with head held high

dark of hue
as if hewn
from darkness

Faxið
glóandi akur

taglið
knippi af korni

His mane
a sunlit field

his tail
a sheaf of corn

31

Augu drengsins
úr dimmu gleri
en brosið minnti
á bræður mína

Of dark glass
were the envoy's eyes,
but the smile brought to mind
my brothers

Þeir biðu eftir
soðningunni

Ég segði þeim líka
sögu af fáknum

They would be waiting
for the fish to boil

To them I would tell
the story of the steed

Bolmikill
brjóstið djúpt
eyrun breið
lendin löng

with its sturdy build
its depth of breast
its breadth of ear
its length of loin

Þegar hófar skullu
á klöppum
var sem bein brysti

The clattering of hooves
on the slabs of rock
was like breaking of bones

Rödd Skírnis
reis yfir rökkvuð trén

Skírnir's voice rose
over dusk-covered trees

Freyr stalst
í stól Óðins

horfði um heima
fékk augastað á mér

Lófar mínir lýstu
löngun hans óx

The god Freyr stole
into Óðinn's throne

looking over all worlds
his eye fell on me

My palms shone bright
as his longing grew

Ástin reikaði
ráðvillt um

soltin, þögul
þyldi hvergi við

His love had gone reeling
in mad career

not eating, not speaking
he would find no rest

Beðið væri
eftir brúði

Nú skyldi
tvímennt
úr tröllaheimi

What was awaited
now was a bride

From giantland
on horseback
two were to ride

Nei

Ég kaus að vera
um kyrrt
þar sem ég þekkti
hverja dæld
og drag

árnar runnu
um æðar mér

No

I would stay
I chose to remain
in the place where I knew
every cranny
and creek

and the rivers ran
through my every vein

Skírnir seiddi fram
sögu af lognblíðu landi
með laufguðum skógi

Gullepli á greinum

Mætti bjóða mér bita?

Skírnir spun a tale
of a land of sweet calm
with a leafy-branched forest

bearing apples of gold

Would I care for a bite?

41

Nei

Hann stæði
fastur í hálsi mér

No

It would only
stick fast in my throat

Þá bauð Skírnir
hring
en mig skorti
ekki skartið

Næga bauga fékk ég
frá föður mínum

What Skírnir then offered
to me was a ring
but of rings for my fingers
of finery too

I had had gifts in full
from my father

Þytur lék um
þokusokkið kjarr

Röddin varð að
reiðu hvæsi

Glerið í
augunum brast

A howl then resounded
through the mist-hung thicket

The voice grew into
an angry hiss

and there came a crack
in the glass of those eyes

Ástin komin
með alvæpni

Drengurinn dró fram
sverð hert í hatri

skeftið skorið úr grimmd

Love had indeed come
armed to the teeth

with an envoy brandishing
a hate-infused sword

its haft carved in cruelty

Sverðið söng
yfir höfði mér
vísu um stelpu
sem stimpast við
og deyr

Hálsinn skreyttur skurði

Over my head
the sword sang a song
the song of a maiden
who struggles
and dies

her neck decked with a slash

46

Sverðið söng um
drengi sem deyja
með kvöl fyrir kodda
óttann ofinn í línið

The sword sang still further
of young men who die
with pain for their pillow
in sheets lined with fear

Feður með stubba
í handa stað
greinar keyrðar
í gapandi sár

augun tínd
úr tóttum
hent fyrir hunda

of fathers with stumps
where their hands should have been
branches driven
into gaping wounds

of eyes torn
from sockets
and thrown to dogs

Ég skyldi dvelja
ein og ástlaus
á arnarþúfu

My penalty to dwell
alone and loveless
on an eagle's perch

Horfa til Heljar

inn í
örfoka land
hinna dauðu

with my gaze towards Hel
the abode of death

towards
the barren
land of the dead

Drottningin
illskeytt
ævaforn

Andlitið
tært upp
af hatri
að hálfu

                                        towards Hel
                                        its queen
                                        evil and ancient

                                        her face
                                        half eaten
                                        away
                                        with hatred

Munnurinn
gapandi gröf

bárust
þaðan vein
týndra og tregaðra

her mouth
a gaping grave

and issuing from it
the baleful wailing
of the lost and mourned

Hún hjó
uppgjöfinni
í hjarta mér

og hló að mér
um leið

Into my heart
she struck
surrender

mocking me
the while

Óðara læstu
tíkur þrjár
í mig tönnum:

Sorg
Einsemd
Þjáning

With rapid bounds
three bitches caught me
fast in their teeth:

Sorrow
Solitude
Suffering

54

Hótanir féllu
sem hagl af himni

Enginn kæmi
að sjá mig

nema þríhöfða þurs

Threats came falling
like hail from the sky

No-one would come
to pay me a visit

save a monster with three heads

Dagar mínir
drumbar í kesti

My days would amount
to logs in a pile

Skírnir ákallaði
þjóð mína og æsi
svo allir vissu
af vesöld minni

Skírnir called out
to my people, to the gods
so that none knew not
of my wretched state

Skelfingin
skorðaðist
í kviði mínum

þandist út
og þyngdist

Bjarg sem
breiddi úr sér

Terror
took hold
in my innermost parts

spreading out,
weighing heavy

a boulder
breaking its bounds

Ég lofaði að koma

Dauðan leit ég
svip minn
í sverði drengsins

I said yes, I would come

and I saw my face,
dead, reflected
in the envoy's sword

Níu nætur

Níu nátta
ótti

Ein tók við
af annarri

Ávallt verri
en sú fyrri

Nine nights

nine nights' worth
of fear

one night
after the other

each worse
than the last

Bræður mínir
og faðir
fögnuðu lífgjöfinni

My brothers
and father
welcomed this gift of life

Gleðin ómaði
um skóga
tyllti sér á trén
tróð sér oní mosann

Joy resounded
through forests
settling on trees
delving into moss

Máni stjakaði
flekum
yfir myrkurhvolf

The moon launched
its rafts
on the vault of darkness

Ég lét fallast
í grasið

grófst í mold

niður

I let myself fall
in a heap in the grass

burrowed into the earth

descending

Niður
fyllti hlustir

the descent roaring
in the portals of my ears

Ég kafaði
undir klettarætur

skaust upp úr
skorningum

gekk yfir
járnfrosna jökla

I dived
deep under rocks

then sprang
from gullies,

walked over stretches
of ice hard as iron

Húðin
tærðist

marðist kjöt
af muldum beinum

skin wasting away,

flesh bruised and broken
from crushing of bones

68

Augu mín
héldu áfram

lontur sem lýstu

My eyes
peered ahead

flickering like fish

Ég lagði á minnið
stapa og strýtur

snjókorn í lófa

I committed to memory
cliffs and peaked crags

snowflakes in my hand

Níunda nóttin

sáust ekki
stjarna hennar skil

When the ninth night came

the stars no longer knew
their stations

Í myrkrinu miðju

mamma

In the midst of the darkness

my mother

Hún vafði mig
örmum

bað mig
að birtast sér aftur

enfolded me
in her arms

conjured me to appear
before her once more

í skugga sem skriði
undan kletti

í mistri
í morgunskógi

in a shade that glided
from under a rock

in the mist
of a forest at dawn

Það dagaði

drengurinn
var kominn

hann kippti mér
upp á klárinn

veröldin vaggaði
undir mér

By break of day

the envoy had come

he hustled me onto the back
of the hack

beneath me the world
went a-rocking

Land mitt laut
þessu hrossi
bauð því stað
að stökkva af

spyrna í spellreið

My country yielded
to this horse,
cleared a way
for its springboard, its leap,

for its desperate, hoof-kicking ride

Nóttin

hylur
að henda sér út í

The night was naught

but a river's deep pool,
into which to plunge

Myrkrið skóf
yfir hjarta mér

Blesa á hesti
blys sem lýsti

the darkness a crust
enclosing my heart

the blaze on the horse's head
a beacon that gleamed

Riðum skriður

Óðum blóðöldur

Over landslides we rode

waded waves of blood

Földu land mitt
feldmjúk ský

Heimur minn horfinn
hefur ekkert
til hans spurst

My homeland was hidden
in clouds soft as fur

My world, since it vanished
has given of itself
not so much as a hint

frekar en gjólu
sem eitt sinn
lék í lokkum
blés þeim frá brosi

læddist lófi í annan

or no more than a gust
which just once, in play,
blew the tresses aside
to reveal a smile

as one hand slipped into another

Mamma

ber lykla að búri
og brjóstum manna

Mother

holds the keys to the pantry
and to human hearts

Augun slæða
gapandi gjótur
þreifa þokuslungin björg

Afdrif mín ókunn

Her eyes scour
cavernous hollows
straining after rocks
wrapped in fog

my destiny unknown

Mamma

birtist í draumum
sem dalalæða
léttir um leið og svefn

Mother

appears in dreams
like mist on a hillside
receding as sleep recedes

Mamma

bíður mín heima
í hamingjunnar bænum

Mother

awaits me at home
at home, by all that is holy!

Ég fór af baki
fylgdist með strák
spretta af hesti

I stepped down from my mount
watched while the horseman
unsaddled the horse

Dauðan leit ég
svip minn í
auga dýrsins

I saw my face
dead, reflected
in the animal's eye

Skírnir brá sverði
brosandi á loft
lagði drauga
og dánar hetjur
skylmdist við skugga

Skírnir drew his sword
smiling skywards
laid low ghosts
and long-dead heroes,
fencing with phantasms

Sverðið
spegill sálarinnar

the sword
a mirror of the soul

Óravíðir akrar
í glóandi sól

Öxin hvísluðu
í golunni:

„Lán þitt engu líkt"

Wide-stretching fields
in glowing sunlight

the ears of corn
whispered in the breeze:

'No luck like yours'

Þó sat ormur
í brjósti mér
og nagaði vonarfjötur

But in my breast
lay a serpent gnawing
at the harness of hope

Freyr stóð
við gerðið

úlfgrá augun
eltu mig

There stood Freyr
by the fence-enclosed field

the wolf-grey eyes
pursued me

Hann vafði
hári mínu
um hönd sér
og leiddi mig

burt

He wrapped
my hair
around his hand
and led me

away

Bærinn
reistur úr
raunum

Þakið úr
þögn

Innviðir
klæddir illsku

to his residence
wrought of
wretchedness

roofed with
reticence

its timbers spliced
with spite

Dagur að
kvöl kominn

Evil the evening
that the day had reached

Vígtennt myrkrið
skreið yfir
himinhvolfið

Sabre-toothed darkness
prowled through
the firmament

Hrammar Freys
hremmdu mig

fleygðu mér
innst í óttann

Freyr's paws
pawed me

reducing me
to terror

Hann risti
sár í svörð
nýtt á hverri nóttu

scored
a new scar
on my skin each night

Líkaminn sveik

lét undan
hörku og spörkum

My body faltered

in the face
of blows and kicks

Rifin út
á röngunni
rimpað saman
jafnharðan

no sooner
ripped apart
than cobbled
together

En líkaminn
heldur
andlitinu

Líkaminn
heldur
áfram

Líkaminn
heldur

Yet the body
holds
its own

The body
holds
firm

The body
holds

Ég lá ein
í úlfabæli
með bitför
í bringu

I lay alone
in a wolf's lair
with marks of bites
on my breast

Hlustaði
eftir hljóðum

Hneggi úr haga

Tipli á
tréfjölum

I listened
for sounds

for a neigh
from the pasture

for a patter
on wooden boards

Kona
strauk mér
um vanga

lét epli
í lófa

A woman
stroked me
on the cheek

put an apple
in my hand

Við fyrsta bita
barst ég niður
gríðarfljót í glerkistu

árarnar
feysknir fluguvængir
flutu burt

Biting it, I was borne
down a mighty river
in a glass casket

the oars,
faded fly's wings,
just floated away

Mamma

hljóp eftir
bakkanum

Ég hrökk upp
við hrópin

Mother

ran along
the bank

startling me
with her cries

Var aftur ein

fékk mig
hvergi hreyft

I was once more alone

in no way
could I move

Fótur fastur
undir stól

Hönd úti
í horni

Fingurnir dreifðir
um gólfið

with a foot stuck fast
under a chair

a hand
in the far corner

fingers all over the floor

Ég safnaði
mér saman

Rétti af brúnir
raðaði tönnum
reyrði inn lifur
og lungu

hnoðaði hjartað
í gang

I gathered myself
into one piece

aligned my eyebrows
set my jaw
tucked in
my liver and lungs

pressed my heart
into service

Í gættinni
mætti ég Frey

Dauðan leit hann
svip sinn í
auga mínu

In the doorway
I met Freyr

He saw his face,
dead, reflected
in my eye

Síðan hefur hann
haldið sig fjarri

fer einförum

He has since kept
his distance

walking alone

Horfir á
hestinn bíta

strýkur yfir
snoppu
vopnlausri hendi

iðrast
skiptanna við Skírni

gazing at his horse
grazing

stroking its muzzle
with a weaponless hand

regretting his dealings
with Skírnir

Sjálf varð ég bústin
og borðaði vel

Ég strekktist
yfir strák

But I grew fat
eating to feed

a boy encased
in my taut-skinned belly

Barn
sem fæddist í blíðviðri

með lófafylli
af sól

a child
born in mild weather

with sunlight
in his hand

Ég hóf hann
til himna

Vindurinn mótaði
skýin í mynd hans

feykti yfir
í jötunheim

Heim!

I held him up
to the skies

The wind formed the clouds
in his image

blowing towards giantland

homewards!

Sjáðu, mamma, son minn!

Fagur sem fiskur í sjó!

Lítill og loðbrýndur
með úlfgrá augu

Mother, behold my son!

Sleek as a sea-fish!

Tiny, with hairy brows
and wolf-grey eyes

Nóttin breiðir
bláma sinn
yfir sveitir

Sonur minn vakir
vill ekki sofa

Night spreads
its blue veil
over hill and dale

My son lies awake
unwilling to sleep

Ég tek hann
í fangið

ferðast yfir
akra og engi

I take him
in my arms

carry him
over cornfields and meadows

Vindur blakar
væng sínum
yfir stráin

Öldurnar fálma
upp á ströndina

The wind flaps
its wing on
the blades of grass

The waves paw away
at the foreshore

Í flæðarmáli
fagur stóll

Útskorinn eðalgripur
með dýrum og
drekahöfðum

On the shoreline stands
a handsome throne

a noble object, carved
with beasts and
dragons' heads

Þau hvæsa að
ég komi og hvílist
með barnið mitt blíða

Hissing, they offer me
a haven of rest
with my beloved son

Við köstum mæði
í mjúku sæti

horfum saman
um heima alla

Sonur minn og ég

Cushioned in that seat
we catch our breath

the two of us looking
over all worlds

my son and I

Heimfús
stefnir hugur minn

yfir vorstillt vatn

járnfrosinn jökul

.

It's homewards with longing
that my heart flies on

over water calmed by spring

over iron-hard ice-fields

125

Ég bíð
endalokanna

Frændur munu
flykkjast yfir brúna

hefna
horfinna kvenna

and I wait
for the end to come

My kinsmen will flock
across the bridge

seeking revenge
for their womenfolk lost

Ég vona að þeir
þekki son minn
og þyrmi honum

sem fékk ég þeim
hlíft forðum daga

I hope that my kin
will acknowledge my son
and spare him

just as I kept them safe
in days of old

Ég vef drenginn
í voð

þrýsti honum
að hjarta mér

I swaddle my boy
in swathing cloth

huddle him
to my heart

Þar er landið mitt
vafið náttkyrri værð

There is my homeland
wrapped in calm of night

steypt í stálkaldan ís

steeped in steel-cold ice

BIOGRAPHICAL NOTES

GERÐUR KRISTNÝ was born in 1970 and brought up in Reykjavík and graduated in French and Comparative Literature from the University of Iceland in 1992. She is now a full-time writer.

Gerður Kristný has published poetry, short stories, novels and books for children, and a biography *Myndin af pabba – Saga Thelmu* (A Portrait of Dad – Thelma's Story) for which she won the Icelandic Journalism Award in 2005.

Other awards for her work include the Children's Choice Book Prize in 2003 for *Marta Smarta* (Smart Martha), the Halldór Laxness Literary Award in 2004 for her novel *Bátur með segli og allt* (A Boat With a Sail and All) and the West-Nordic Children's Literature Prize in 2010 for the novel *Garðurinn* (The Garden).

Her collection of poetry, *Höggstaður* (Soft Spot), was nominated for the Icelandic Literature Prize in 2007 and she then won the prize in 2010 for her poetry book *Blóðhófnir* (Bloodhoof).

Gerður Kristný lives in Reykjavík but travels regularly around the world to present her work.

RORY MCTURK graduated from Oxford in 1963, took a further degree at the University of Iceland, Reykjavík in 1965, and after teaching at the universities of Lund and Copenhagen, and then University College, Dublin, took up a post at Leeds University in 1978.

In addition to his two authored books, *Studies in Ragnars Saga Loðbrókar and its Major Scandinavian Analogues* (Oxford, 1991) and *Chaucer and the Norse and Celtic Worlds* (Aldershot, 2005), he has edited the *Blackwell Companion to Old Norse-Icelandic Literature and Culture* (Oxford, 2004), and co-edited, with Andrew Wawn, a volume of essays, *Úr Dölum til Dala* (Leeds, 1989) in commemoration of the Icelandic scholar Guðbrandur Vigfússon (1827-89). He has also contributed five edited texts to *A New Introduction to Old Norse, Part II, Reader* (5th edition, ed. Anthony Faulkes, London, 2011).

His publications also include two Icelandic saga translations, two book-length translations of scholarly works on Icelandic topics (one from Swedish, the other from Icelandic), numerous essays and articles in journals, and a translation (published in 2007) of an Icelandic novel, *The Thief of Time*, by Steinunn Sigurðardóttir (Reykjavík, 1986).

Arc Publications
publishes translated poetry in bilingual editions
in the following series:

ARC TRANSLATIONS
Series Editor Jean Boase-Beier

'VISIBLE POETS'
Series Editor Jean Boase-Beier

ARC CLASSICS:
NEW TRANSLATIONS OF GREAT POETS OF THE PAST
Series Editor Jean Boase-Beier

ARC ANTHOLOGIES IN TRANSLATION
Series Editor Jean Boase-Beier

NEW VOICES FROM EUROPE & BEYOND
(anthologies)
Series Editor Alexandra Büchler

details of which can be found on the
Arc Publications website at
www.arcpublications.co.uk